P9-AOK-815

CONTEMPORARY'S

Breakthroughs

in Writing and Language

CONTEMPORARY'S

Breakthroughs
in Writing and Language

EXERCISE BOOK

ℭℬ

CONTEMPORARY BOOKS

a division of NTC/CONTEMPORARY PUBLISHING GROUP
Lincolnwood, Illinois USA

ISBN: 0-8092-3299-5

Published by Contemporary Books,
a division of NTC/Contemporary Publishing Group, Inc.,
4255 West Touhy Avenue,
Lincolnwood (Chicago), Illinois 60646-1975 U.S.A.
© 1996 by NTC/Contemporary Publishing Group, Inc.
All rights reserved. No part of this book may be reproduced,
stored in a retrieval system, or transmitted in any form or by any means,
electronic, mechanical, photocopying, recording, or otherwise,
without prior permission of the publisher.
Manufactured in the United States of America.
 9 0 M&G 1 0 9 8 7 6 5

CONTENTS

TO THE STUDENT

Welcome to the *Breakthroughs in Writing and Language Exercise Book*. In this book, you'll be practicing the skills you learned in Contemporary's *Breakthroughs in Writing and Language*. You will work on basic English grammar and usage, and you will write short paragraphs and essays.

Each exercise in this book corresponds to one or more lessons in *Breakthroughs in Writing and Language*. Look for the numbers under "Text Pages" in the margin of each exercise. They will tell you where to learn more about that skill in the Breakthroughs book.

Be sure to check your answers after you finish each exercise in this book. You'll find answers to all the grammar and usage exercises at the back of the book. To check a writing assignment, use the Writing Checklist at the end of each assignment. If you are working with an instructor, you might also ask him or her to look at your writing assignments.

When you have completed the exercises and writing assignments in this book, take the Post-Test. The Post-Test Answer Key on pages 61–62 will help you evaluate your answers. Then fill out the Post-Test Evaluation Chart on page 63. It will tell you what skills you need to review.

Finally, remember that language skills improve with practice. Take advantage of opportunities to practice writing at home, work, and school.

PARTS OF SPEECH

TEXT PAGES
12–13

Nouns

A *noun* names a person, place, thing, or idea.

Person: brother, woman, Carlos, Marla

Place: town, store, First National Bank, Texas

Thing: horse, desk, computer, car

Idea: peace, history, boredom, patience

Part A
Directions: Underline the nouns in each sentence.

EXAMPLE

My <u>sister</u> and <u>brother</u> love <u>music</u>.

1. <u>Lenora</u> can play the <u>trumpet</u>, <u>saxophone</u>, and <u>clarinet</u>.

2. <u>Jack</u> can play the <u>piano</u>, <u>organ</u>, and <u>guitar</u>.

3. <u>Jack</u> and <u>Lenora</u> formed a <u>band</u> with some <u>friends</u>.

4. The <u>band</u> has played in many <u>clubs</u> in <u>Chicago</u> and <u>Detroit</u>.

5. My <u>sister</u> and <u>brother</u> earn good <u>money</u> as <u>musicians</u>.

6. But my <u>parents</u> want <u>Jack</u> and <u>Lenora</u> to go back to <u>school</u>.

7. Their <u>dream</u> is for all their <u>kids</u> to get a good <u>education</u>.

8. Next <u>fall</u> my <u>sister</u> and <u>brother</u> will take some <u>classes</u>.

Part B
Directions: Complete the lists by adding nouns of your choice.

List 1 People You'd Like to Meet	**List 2** Places You'd Like to Visit	**List 3** Things You'd Like to Buy
_____	_____	_____
_____	_____	_____
_____	_____	_____

Check your answers on page 64.

Pronouns

Pronouns are words that take the place of nouns.

I, me, my, mine	you, your, yours
he, him, his	we, us, our, ours
she, her, hers	they, them, their, theirs
it, its	

Part A

Directions: Underline the pronoun or pronouns in each sentence.

EXAMPLE   <u>My</u> friends and <u>I</u> like to read poetry by Gwendolyn Brooks.

1. Have you read her poems?

2. She has won many prizes for them.

3. Our class read some of her poems aloud.

4. She wrote a poem called "We Real Cool."

5. It is about high school dropouts.

6. They play pool and don't care about their future.

7. School isn't important to them.

Part B

Directions: Replace each noun in parentheses with a pronoun.

EXAMPLE   (Red Grange) _He_ was a great football player during the 1920s and early 1930s.

1. In college, (Grange) _____ once scored four touchdowns in the first 12 minutes of a game.

2. (The game) _____ helped make (Grange)_____ a star.

3. After college, (Grange) _____ played for the Chicago Bears.

4. (Fans) _____ flocked to see Grange play.

5. (Grange's) _____ nickname was the "Galloping Ghost."

Check your answers on page 64.

Verbs

A *verb* is a word that shows action or being.

Action verbs: fly, eat, drive, walk, fall

Being (linking) verbs: am, is, are, was, were

Part A
Directions: Underline the verb or verbs in each sentence.

EXAMPLE

Two men <u>robbed</u> a grocery store.

1. The robbers stole $500 from the cash register.

2. One robber pointed a gun at the store owner while the other robber took the money.

3. Police officers raced to the scene of the crime.

4. The store owner described the robbers.

5. Both of them were tall and wore blue jackets.

6. The police searched the store for clues.

7. The store owner was grateful for the officers' help.

Part B
Directions: Imagine that you are a sportscaster. Describe a moment from a football, baseball, or basketball game. Write five sentences that tell what the players are doing. Use at least one action verb in each sentence. Choose verbs from the list or think of your own.

List: bounce, catch, cheer, hit, jump, kick, make, pass, pitch, rise, run, slide, soar, tackle, turn, throw

EXAMPLE

The quarterback throws the ball to a wide receiver.

1. _____

2. _____

3. _____

4. _____

5. _____

Check your answers on page 64.

Adjectives

Adjectives describe nouns by telling which one, what kind, or how many.

Which one: this, that, these, those

What kind: hot, cold, smooth, thin, red

How many: several, some, three, many

Part A

Directions: Underline the adjectives in each sentence.

EXAMPLE

<u>This</u> winter, get away from the <u>deep</u> snow and <u>icy</u> winds.

1. Spend some time in beautiful, sunny Jamaica.

2. Relax on clean, white beaches.

3. Let warm, fragrant breezes caress your skin.

4. Listen to the soothing sound of gentle waves.

5. Treat yourself to these wonderful experiences today.

Part B

Directions: Complete each sentence by adding an adjective of your choice from the correct list.

Which one: these, those

What kind: good, graceful, handsome, happy, lonely, loud, romantic

How many: two, many, several, some

EXAMPLE

The ____*lonely*____ man walked into the house.
        (what kind)

1. A _____ party was in full swing.
        (what kind)

2. _____ music was coming from the stereo.
        (what kind)

3. _____ couples were dancing around the room.
        (how many)

4. Seeing _____ couples dance made the man jealous.
        (which one)

Check your answers on page 64.

Adverbs _____

Adverbs describe verbs. Adverbs can tell how, when, or where.

How: quickly, softly, happily

When: early, late, soon, now

Where: here, there, everywhere

Part A

Directions: Underline the adverb in each sentence. (Answer the question after each sentence to find the adverb.)

EXAMPLE   Lu came to work <u>early</u>.   (*When* did she come?)

1. She neatly typed the important letter.   (*How* did she type it?)

2. Her boss read the letter carefully.   (*How* did he read it?)

3. Lu quickly brought it to the mail room.   (*How* did she bring it?)

4. She left the letter there.   (*Where* did she leave it?)

5. Later the clerk mailed it.   (*When* did he mail it?)

Part B

Directions: Complete each sentence by adding an adverb of your choice from the correct list.

How: confidently, cheerfully, nervously, politely, sweetly

When: soon, later, then

Where: everywhere, here, nearby, there

1. The woman walked _____ into the employment office.
                              (how)

2. A young man sitting _____ began to speak.
                              (where)

3. He said he had looked _____ for a job.
                              (where)

4. _____ the receptionist called out his name.
     (when)

5. As he rose, the young woman _____ said, "Good luck!"
                                       (how)

Check your answers on page 65.

WRITING ASSIGNMENT

AN EVENT IN YOUR LIFE

Directions: On another piece of paper, write a story about an event in your life. Put the story in *time order*—the order in which the event actually happened. Here are some suggestions for topics.

- ✪ My first date
- ✪ My first job interview
- ✪ My best (or worst) experience in school
- ✪ My favorite trip
- ✪ My argument with a relative
- ✪ The birth of my first child

You can choose a different topic to write about. Just be sure to pick a topic that really interests you. When you are finished writing, use the Writing Checklist to look over what you wrote.

☑ WRITING CHECKLIST

- ☐ Have you said everything you wanted to say?
- ☐ Did you use time order to tell about the event?
- ☐ Are there any changes you want to make?

WHAT IS A SENTENCE?

TEXT PAGES
26–28
Identifying Sentences and Fragments _____

A *sentence* is a group of words that expresses a complete thought.

A *fragment* does not express a complete thought.

Part A
Directions: Circle *S* if a group of words is a sentence. Circle *F* if it is a fragment.

EXAMPLE (S) F Shirley Chisholm was an important leader.

S F **1.** Chisholm came from a working-class family.

S F **2.** She knew that the poor faced serious problems.

S F **3.** Wanted to find ways to help.

S F **4.** Chisholm became a member of Congress in 1968.

S F **5.** The first female African-American congressperson.

S F **6.** In 1972, ran for president in several primaries.

S F **7.** Chisholm was the first African-American woman to do so.

S F **8.** Retired from Congress in 1982.

Part B
Directions: Each of the following pairs contains one sentence and one fragment. Underline the fragment.

EXAMPLE Horace Greeley was a famous newspaper editor. <u>Born in 1811.</u>

1. Greeley fought against slavery. Believing it to be wrong.

2. Started the *New York Times*. It was a powerful newspaper.

3. Greeley wrote many editorials. Against the death penalty.

4. Nominated for president by the Liberal Republican party. He died before the election was over.

Check your answers on page 65.

Turning Fragments into Sentences

A *fragment* is an incomplete thought. You can turn a fragment into a sentence by completing the thought.

Directions: All of the following groups of words are fragments. Turn each fragment into a sentence by adding information that completes the thought. To tell which information to add, answer the question after the fragment.

EXAMPLE

Went on a job interview.
(Who went on a job interview?)

The man went on a job interview.

1. Described the job, salary, and benefits.
   (Who described the job, salary, and benefits?)

   _____

2. The person who was hired.
   (What would the person who was hired be doing?)

   _____

3. The salary.
   (What was the salary?)

   _____

4. Receive group health insurance.
   (Who receive group health insurance?)

   _____

5. Was hired for the job.
   (Who was hired for the job?)

   _____

6. Felt happy.
   (Who felt happy and why?)

   _____

Check your answers on page 65.

Types of Sentences

There are four types of sentences. A *statement* gives information. A *command* tells someone to do something. A *question* asks something. An *exclamation* shows strong feeling.

Part A
Directions: Write the correct endmark on the line at the end of each sentence. On the line below, write whether the sentence is a statement, command, question, or exclamation.

EXAMPLE

All of our employees punch a time clock .

statement

1. Do you know how to use the machine __

2. Place your time card inside the slot __

3. The machine stamped the correct time on your card __

4. I forgot to punch out before lunch __

5. Tell the payroll clerk to subtract one hour __

Part B
Directions: Complete each of the following sentences.

EXAMPLE

(Command)   Remember to set your alarm clock.

1. (Question)   How do you _____

2. (Exclamation)   The horror movie _____

3. (Statement)   The new restaurant _____

4. (Command)   Do not _____

Check your answers on page 65.

Mistakes in Sentences

Remember: A *sentence* expresses a complete thought. A *fragment* does not express a complete thought.

Directions: Underline the fragments in the paragraph. Then rewrite the paragraph so that there are no fragments.

EXAMPLE

Many people remember their dreams. <u>After waking up.</u> People of all cultures have long wondered. <u>About the nature of dreams.</u>

Many people remember their dreams after waking up.
People of all cultures have long wondered about the
nature of dreams.

Different cultures have different ideas. About how and why people dream. People in some cultures believe there is a dream world. A place where the soul goes when a person is asleep. These people believe that a person's soul may become lost in the dream world. If he or she is suddenly awakened. As a result, they are careful not to disturb sleepers. People in other cultures believe that events in their dreams are real. These people have been known to end friendships. After dreaming that their friends did them harm. In some cultures, dreams are believed to be clues to the future. People in these cultures may go to a medicine man or other religious leader. For help in figuring out what a dream means.

_____

_____

_____

_____

_____

_____

_____

_____

_____

Check your answers on page 66.

Finding the Subject

To find the *subject* of a sentence, look for the verb. Then ask, Who or what is performing the action? Who or what is the sentence about?

Part A
Directions: Underline the verb twice. Then underline the subject once.

EXAMPLE	Farmers work very hard.

1. Machines help farmers do their jobs.

2. A tractor is an important piece of farm equipment.

3. Plows are heavy machines with blades.

4. The blades loosen the soil.

5. Crops need certain foods for growth.

6. Fertilizers are plant food.

7. Farmers spread fertilizers on the soil.

8. Some insects ruin crops.

9. The locust eats plant leaves.

10. Scientists developed chemicals for killing pests.

11. Some pesticides were poisonous to other living things.

12. People want safer methods of protecting crops.

Part B
Directions: Write three sentences about machines that help people do their jobs. Underline each verb twice and each subject once.

EXAMPLE	Administrative assistants use computers.

1. _____

2. _____

3. _____

Check your answers on page 66.

Finding Tricky Subjects

Be aware of these three structures when looking for subjects.

1. **Commands:** (You) Buy groceries after work.
   The subject of commands is always the word *you*.

2. **Questions:** Did Kala turn off the computer?
   Notice that part of the verb comes before the subject.

3. **Phrases:** [In June], the roses [in my yard] blossom.
   Ignore phrases that do not contain the subject.

Part A
Directions: Underline the subject in each sentence. If a sentence is a command, write the word *you* for the subject.

EXAMPLE   Avoid salty and fatty foods. (you)

1. Why is a good diet important?

2. According to doctors, a good diet can help prevent disease.

3. Do you read the labels on packaged food?

4. The labels on a product may have important information.

5. Read lists of ingredients carefully.

6. Besides ingredients, labels may include other facts.

7. How can you tell the fat content of a packaged food?

8. Look at the label.

Part B
Directions: Complete each of the following sentences.

EXAMPLE   (Command) Drink *plenty of liquids.*

1. (Command) Eat _____

2. (Question) What is _____

3. (Phrase) For breakfast, _____

Check your answers on page 66.

Action and Linking Predicates

The *predicate* of a sentence tells what the subject does or is. To find the predicate, look for an action verb or a linking verb. There is always a verb in the predicate.

Action Predicate: Tony **baked** fudge cookies.

Linking Predicate: The cookies **were** delicious.

Part A

Directions: Complete each predicate by adding an action verb.

EXAMPLES

The temperature _soared_ on the hottest day of the year.

Tires _squealed_ on the burning streets.

1. Dogs _____ under porches to escape the heat.

2. People _____ different ways to cool off.

3. Some people _____ to the beach.

4. Other people _____ their bathing suits at home.

5. Many other people _____ cool drinks.

Part B

Directions: Complete each predicate by adding a linking verb (am, is, are, was, were) and an adjective.

EXAMPLES

Ted _was_ _tired_.

His job _is_ _hard_.

1. I _____ _____.

2. My boss _____ _____.

3. The photographs _____ _____.

4. Some movies _____ _____.

5. The new building _____ _____.

6. That rap group _____ _____.

Check your answers on page 66.

WRITING ASSIGNMENT

MAKING A WORD PICTURE

Directions: On another piece of paper, write a paragraph describing a place. Try to include sights, sounds, smells, textures, and tastes in your paragraph. Here are some places that you might write about.

- ✪ A place from your childhood
- ✪ Your home
- ✪ Your favorite restaurant
- ✪ A park
- ✪ The waiting room of a dentist's office
- ✪ A school gym during a basketball game

You can choose a different place to write about. Just be sure to pick a place that really interests you. When you are finished writing, use the Writing Checklist to look over what you wrote.

☑ WRITING CHECKLIST

- ☐ Have you used details to describe your place?
- ☐ Have you checked your spelling?
- ☐ Is the first letter of every sentence capitalized?
- ☐ Is there a punctuation mark at the end of every sentence?

NOUNS AND PRONOUNS

TEXT PAGES
46–49

Capitalizing Proper Nouns

Capitalize *proper nouns*—specific names of people, places, things, and ideas. Do not capitalize *common nouns*—general names of people, places, things, and ideas.

Proper Nouns: Michael Jordan, Brownsville, Labor Day, Korean War

Common Nouns: basketball player, city, holiday, war

Part A
Directions: Capitalize the proper noun or nouns in each sentence.

EXAMPLE

On November 22, 1963, President John F. Kennedy was killed.

1. He was riding in an open car in dallas.

2. As the car turned left on elm street, shots were fired.

3. The car raced to dallas parkland hospital, but kennedy was hurt too badly to be saved.

4. The governor of texas, john b. connally, also was wounded.

5. President kennedy was buried at arlington national cemetery in washington, d.c.

6. Most americans mourned his death.

7. During the 1991 christmas season, a movie about the murder opened in theaters.

8. The name of the movie is *jfk*.

Part B
Directions: Capitalize the proper nouns.

Abraham lincoln served as president during the civil war. On april 14, 1865, he and his wife went to ford's theater to see a play. During the play, john wilkes booth shot and killed president lincoln.

Check your answers on page 67.

Forming Plural Nouns

Plural nouns name more than one person, place, thing, or idea. Most nouns form the plural with the letter *s*: one hat, two hats.

1. Nouns ending in *s*, *sh*, *ch*, *z*, and *x* take an *es* ending.
    one bru<u>sh</u>, two brush<u>es</u>

2. Nouns ending in a consonant and *y* take an *ies* ending.
    one compa<u>ny</u>, two compan<u>ies</u>

3. Irregular nouns may change spelling, take an unusual ending, or undergo no change at all.
    one m<u>a</u>n, two m<u>en</u>; one ox, two ox<u>en</u>; one sheep, two sheep

Part A
Directions: Underline the plural error in each sentence. Write the correct plural form above the line.

                                                groups
There are many religious <u>group</u> in the United States.

The Amish are a group with strong religious belief. They pray regularly in their churchs. The Amish don't live in large citys. They live in small communitys. The Amish live by strict rule. Amish woman wear caps and shawls in public. The mens wear hats most of the time. The childs don't watch TV or talk on the phone. The Amish ride in horse-drawn buggys instead of cars.

Part B
Directions: Write the plural of each of these singular nouns.

1. box

2. factory

3. person

4. attorney

5. desk

Check your answers on page 67.

Possessive Nouns

A noun that shows ownership is a *possessive noun*.

1. To make a singular noun possessive, add *'s*.
That girl's coat is unusual.

2. To make a plural noun ending in *s* possessive, add an *'*.
The store has a sale on girls' shoes.

3. To make an irregular noun possessive, add *'s*.
Men's, women's, and children's shoes are on sale.

Part A
Directions: Write the possessive form of each noun.

EXAMPLE

a car owned by Pedro

Pedro's car

1. tools owned by carpenters

_____

2. a bottle belonging to a baby

_____

3. an office belonging to a doctor

_____

4. advice of friends

_____

5. rights of women

_____

Part B
Directions: Underline and correct the possessive noun errors.

EXAMPLE

principal's
The principals office was filled with angry parents.

They wanted the teachers strike to end. Their childrens education was at

stake. Many students went to their friends houses during the day. The

schools bus drivers were also losing money.

Check your answers on page 67.

Subject and Object Pronouns

Subject pronouns (*I, you, he, she, it, we, they*) take the place of nouns that are subjects. *Object pronouns* (*me, you, him, her, it, them, us*) take the place of nouns that are not subjects.

Part A
Directions: On the blank line, write the pronoun that can take the place of the underlined words.

EXAMPLE ___she___   Has <u>Rosa</u> ever seen a mural?

_____ **1.** <u>A mural</u> is a painting done on a wall.

_____ **2.** <u>Murals</u> are a popular form of art.

_____ **3.** Some Mexican artists paint <u>murals</u>.

_____ **4.** <u>Diego Rivera</u> was a master of the form.

_____ **5.** <u>Eva and I</u> saw a mural on the side of a church.

_____ **6.** <u>Eva</u> liked the bright colors and bold shapes.

_____ **7.** Benito told <u>Eva and me</u> where to find other murals.

_____ **8.** Eva got specific directions from <u>Benito</u>.

_____ **9.** I went with <u>Eva</u> to look at the murals.

_____ **10.** <u>You and your friends</u> should go too.

Part B
Directions: Write two sentences using subject pronouns and two sentences using object pronouns. Underline each pronoun.

EXAMPLE <u>I</u> love fast food. _____

1. _____

2. _____

3. _____

4. _____

Check your answers on page 67.

Possessive Pronouns

Possessive pronouns take the place of possessive nouns. The following possessive pronouns appear with a noun to show who or what owns something: *my, your, his, her, its, our, their.* The following possessive pronouns can stand alone: *mine, yours, his, hers, its, ours, theirs.*

Part A
Directions: On the blank line, write the possessive pronoun that can take the place of the underlined word or words.

EXAMPLE   _his_   Did you hear about <u>Misha's</u> new job?

_____ **1.** He is <u>Mr. Johnson's</u> assistant.

_____ **2.** Misha works in <u>the company's</u> sales department.

_____ **3.** He takes <u>customers'</u> orders over the phone.

_____ **4.** The desk next to the computer is <u>Misha's</u>.

_____ **5.** <u>My job</u> also involves phone work.

_____ **6.** I take <u>people's</u> phone reservations for concerts.

_____ **7.** What skills are required for <u>Misha's job and mine</u>?

_____ **8.** What skills are required for <u>your job</u>?

Part B
Directions: Write a sentence for each possessive pronoun in parentheses.

EXAMPLE   (ours) _The new computer is ours._

1. (your) _____

2. (yours) _____

3. (theirs) _____

4. (its) _____

5. (mine) _____

Check your answers on page 67.

Contractions and Possessive Pronouns _____

A *contraction* is formed when two words are combined into one. An apostrophe (') shows where any letters in a contraction have been left out. Apostrophes are never used in possessive pronouns.

You're getting a raise. (*You're* is short for *you are*.)
You deserve your raise. (*Your* is a possessive pronoun.)

Part A
Directions: On the blank line, write the contraction for the underlined words.

EXAMPLE *can't*   Delores and Joseph <u>cannot</u> come to the party.

_____ **1.** <u>They are</u> going out of town.

_____ **2.** I know <u>you are</u> coming.

_____ **3.** Ask Larry if <u>he will</u> bring his tapes.

_____ **4.** Nick <u>does not</u> like blues.

_____ **5.** Laurie promised that she <u>would not</u> be late.

_____ **6.** <u>I am</u> ordering pizza for the party.

_____ **7.** <u>It is</u> from Roma's Pizza Parlor.

_____ **8.** <u>That is</u> everyone's favorite restaurant.

_____ **9.** I <u>do not</u> have time to cook for so many people.

_____ **10.** <u>We will</u> all have a great time.

Part B
Directions: Underline and correct the contraction or possessive pronoun error in each sentence.

EXAMPLE
Your
<u>You're</u> children are starting school next week.

Did they get they're shots? My son is in you're daughter's class. I know its hard raising children by yourself. Ive been a single parent for three years. Lets have lunch sometime.

Check your answers on page 68.

WRITING ASSIGNMENT

A ONE-SIDED ARGUMENT

Directions: Imagine that you are having an argument with someone about a given topic. On another piece of paper, explain where you stand on the issue—either for or against. Give reasons to support your opinion. Here are some suggestions for topics.

- ✪ Companies should provide day-care centers for their employees' children.

- ✪ Companies should require all employees to be tested for drugs.

- ✪ The fathers of newborn babies should get time off from their jobs.

- ✪ Women should not fight in wars.

You can choose a different issue to write about. Just be sure to pick a topic that you really know about. When you are finished writing, use the Writing Checklist to look over what you wrote.

☑ WRITING CHECKLIST

☐ Does every sentence support your opinion?

☐ Are all plural nouns spelled correctly?

☐ Did you use pronouns and contractions correctly?

VERBS: FORM AND TENSE

TEXT PAGES
70–73

Choosing Present Tense Verbs

Verb tenses tell when an action happens. The ***present tense*** is used to show that something takes place regularly.

The sun <u>rises</u> in the east and <u>sets</u> in the west.

Add the letter *s* to the end of a present tense verb when it goes with one of these subjects: *he, she, it.* Do not add an *s* when the verb goes with one of these subjects: *I, you, we, they.*

<u>She works</u> three days a week. <u>I work</u> full-time.

Directions: Underline the subject in each sentence. Then underline the correct verb form in parentheses.

EXAMPLE

<u>Michael</u> (see, <u>sees</u>) Dr. Vicki Yung once a year.

1. The doctor (listen, listens) to his heart.

2. She (put, puts) a stethoscope on his chest.

3. Michael's heart (make, makes) a noise like a drum.

4. The heart (work, works) like a pump.

5. The average adult heart (pump, pumps) the equivalent of about 5,000 quarts of blood each day.

6. Normal hearts (weigh, weighs) less than a pound.

7. Arteries (carry, carries) blood away from the heart.

8. They (resemble, resembles) long, narrow tubes.

9. Veins (move, moves) blood back to the heart.

10. Dr. Yung (take, takes) blood from Michael's veins.

11. The blood from his veins (look, looks) dark red.

12. Lab technicians (examine, examines) the blood under a microscope.

Check your answers on page 68.

Past and Future Tenses of Regular Verbs _____

The *past tense* shows that an action has already happened. Form the past tense of most regular verbs by adding an *ed* ending. If the verb ends in *e*, add *d* to form the past tense. The *future tense* shows that something will take place at a later date. Form this tense by adding the helping verb *will* in front of the verb.

Part A
Directions: Write the past tense of each verb in parentheses.

EXAMPLE

In 1969, people (land**ed**) on the moon for the first time.

1. Neil Armstrong and Buzz Aldrin (walk   ) on its surface.

2. They (plant   ) the American flag firmly in the ground.

3. Then they (salute   ) the flag.

4. Armstrong (describe   ) the moon.

5. The moon (look   ) like a huge desert.

6. Americans (watch   ) the astronauts on TV.

7. President Nixon (talk   ) to the men on a special phone.

8. The astronauts (enjoy   ) their time on the moon.

9. Because there was little gravity, they (jump   ) around easily.

10. They (stay   ) on the moon for about two hours.

Part B
Directions: Write the past and future tenses of each verb.

Base Verb	Past Tense	Future Tense
cook	cooked	will cook
1. roast		
2. bake		
3. boil		
4. prepare		
5. mash		

Check your answers on page 68.

Past Tense of Irregular Verbs

In the past tense, *irregular verbs* do not take an *ed* ending. Instead, they change spelling.

Base Verb	Past Tense
know	knew
begin	began
send	sent
break	broke

Part A
Directions: Write the past tense of each verb above the parentheses.

EXAMPLE

Lou Gehrig (grow) *grew* up in New York.

1. He (become) a member of the New York Yankees.

2. He (win) the American League's Most Valuable Player award.

3. Gehrig (lead) the league in home runs three times.

4. In June 1939, Gehrig (find) out he had a fatal disease.

5. On Independence Day of 1939, Gehrig (stand) before his fans.

6. He (speak) into a microphone at Yankee Stadium.

7. He (tell) everyone about his illness.

8. Gehrig (fight) back the tears.

9. The fans (feel) sad about the terrible news.

10. Baseball (lose) one of its greatest players.

Part B
Directions: Write the past tense of each underlined verb.

EXAMPLE

During the summer, Jesse *went* <u>goes</u> to baseball games.

He <u>has</u> season tickets. He usually <u>takes</u> Molly with him. They <u>buy</u> hot dogs and <u>sit</u> in the upper deck. They <u>get</u> mad when their favorite players <u>strike</u> out.

Check your answers on page 68.

Forms of *Be*

The linking verb *be* is very irregular. Its form changes for different subjects in both the present and past tenses.

Subject	Present	Past
I	am	was
he, she, it	is	was
we, you, they	are	were

Part A
Directions: Underline the correct verb form in parentheses.

EXAMPLE

Many banks (be, <u>are</u>) concerned about disabled customers.

1. They (is, are) trying to give them special services.

2. One bank (is, are) teaching its employees sign language.

3. Before, nobody (was, were) able to help deaf customers.

4. People in wheelchairs also (was, were) overlooked.

5. Cash machines (was, were) designed for people who can stand.

6. A new machine (was, were) built for people in wheelchairs.

7. Some cash machines (is, are) even able to help blind people.

8. They (is, are) made with computer voices to help the blind.

9. I (was, were) amazed by all the new services at my bank.

Part B
Directions: Underline and correct the being verb error in each sentence.

EXAMPLE

TV talk shows <u>is</u> interesting.
are

We was watching a television show. A young man be interviewing other single men. A young woman were asking for their phone numbers. I is going to watch tomorrow's show. The guests is going to be soap opera stars.

Check your answers on pages 68–69.

Forms of *Have* and *Do*

Two of the most common irregular verbs are *have* and *do*.

Subject	Present	Past	Future
I, you, we, they	have, do	had, did	will have, will do
he, she, it	has, does	had, did	will have, will do

Part A

Directions: Write the correct form of *have* for each sentence.

EXAMPLE

(present)   Mario and Angela _have_ many books.

1. (future)   They _____ time to read this weekend.

2. (present)   Mario _____ a book of Sherlock Holmes stories.

3. (present)   Holmes _____ an assistant named Watson.

4. (present)   They always _____ crimes to solve.

5. (past)   One story _____ a plot about a mysterious murder.

6. (past)   Holmes _____ clues to help him solve the case.

7. (present)   Angela _____ an interest in science fiction.

Part B

Directions: Write the correct form of *do* for each sentence.

EXAMPLE

(present)   _Do_ you organize your time well?

1. (present)   Efficient employees _____ more work.

2. (past)   Last week, Sheila _____ a schedule for her work.

3. (past)   She _____ all her tasks on time.

4. (future)   Tomorrow, Ed _____ a department schedule.

5. (present)   He _____ not want anyone to waste time.

6. (present)   _____ you have a wall calendar?

7. (past)   If you _____, you could organize your time.

Check your answers on page 69.

Time Clues to Verb Tenses

Words and phrases like *now, this minute,* and *today* are **time clues** that tell you something is happening in the present. Time clues like *yesterday, last year,* and *a few weeks ago* tell you something happened in the past. Time clues like *tomorrow, in three hours,* and *next year* tell you something will happen in the future.

Part A

Directions: Underline the time clue in each sentence. Then write the correct form of the verb.

EXAMPLE   (want)   <u>Today</u>, many people __want__ to quit smoking.

1. (think)   Years ago, people _____ smoking was OK.

2. (know)   Now, doctors _____ cigarettes are harmful.

3. (allow)   In the past, airlines _____ in-flight smoking.

4. (ban)   Nowadays, airlines _____ smoking during flights.

5. (smoke)   Last year, Cecilia _____ a pack a day.

6. (attend)   Next week, she _____ a class to help her stop smoking.

7. (take)   Her company's no-smoking rule _____ effect in a few weeks.

8. (prohibit)   In the future, most companies _____ smoking.

Part B

Directions: Write sentences using present, past, and future tense verbs. Begin each sentence with the time clue in parentheses.

EXAMPLE   (Now) <u>Now most people exercise.</u>

1. (Today)   _____

2. (Yesterday)   _____

3. (Last year)   _____

4. (Tomorrow)   _____

Check your answers on page 69.

The Continuing Tenses

The *present continuing tense* is formed by using *am*, *is*, or *are* as a helping verb with the base verb plus *ing*.

What <u>are</u> you <u>doing</u>? I <u>am talking</u> on the phone.

The *past continuing tense* is formed by using *was* or *were* as a helping verb with the base verb plus *ing*.

What <u>were</u> you <u>doing</u> when I called? I <u>was taking</u> a bath.

Part A
Directions: Underline the correct verb form in parentheses. Make sure that the verb you choose agrees with the subject.

EXAMPLE

Fewer people (is, <u>are</u>) going to movie theaters.

1. The price of a ticket (is, are) getting expensive.

2. Videos (is, are) becoming more popular.

3. I (am, is) watching a science fiction movie.

4. Carla (am, is) watching it with me.

5. Monsters (is, are) leaving the spaceship.

6. Carla and I (is, are) enjoying the incredible story.

Part B
Directions: Underline the correct verb form in parentheses. Make sure that the verb you choose agrees with the subject.

1. U.S. family life (was, were) changing during the late 1800s.

2. Many families (was, were) moving from the farm to the city.

3. City life (was, were) affecting the family.

4. Men (was, were) working in factories, shops, and offices.

5. More women (was, were) beginning to work outside the home.

6. The average parent (was, were) spending less time at home.

Check your answers on page 69.

Using Quotation Marks _____

When you repeat the exact words that someone used, set the words off with *quotation marks*.

"I'll get tickets for the baseball game," said Ray.
Sylvia asked, "How much do the tickets cost?"

Directions: Add quotation marks to the following conversation.

EXAMPLE   Arnie said, "I read a good article in today's newspaper."

1. What was the article about? John asked.

2. Arnie replied, It's about children playing sports.

3. My ten-year-old, Bobby, plays on a football team, John said.

4. According to the article, he shouldn't, Arnie said.

5. John asked, What are the reasons?

6. Arnie answered, His body isn't developed enough.

7. But Bobby is big for his age! John explained.

8. Arnie warned, It's still risky because he could get injured.

9. John remarked, A teammate of Bobby's did break a leg.

10. Many athletes his age break bones, said Arnie.

11. Arnie added, Some children put too much pressure on themselves.

12. Bobby does get very upset when the team loses, John admitted.

13. Doctors think that young children should play sports just for the fun of it, Arnie said.

14. Arnie asked, What do you think?

15. Maybe they're right, John replied.

Check your answers on pages 69–70.

W R I T I N G   A S S I G N M E N T

TELLING A STORY

Directions: On another piece of paper, write a story about a funny experience you have had. Think about these questions as you write the story:

- ✪ Where and when did the experience take place?

- ✪ What happened?

- ✪ Who were the people involved in the situation?

- ✪ What did the people say?

When you are finished writing, use the Writing Checklist to look over what you wrote.

☑ W R I T I N G   C H E C K L I S T

☐ Did you include all the important details?

☐ Did you use the correct form of all verb tenses?

☐ Did you put quotation marks around all direct quotations?

SUBJECT-VERB AGREEMENT

TEXT PAGES
98–99

Pronouns as Subjects

A verb and its subject are said to **agree** when the verb is in the right form for the subject. In the present tense, a verb must end in *s* when the subject is *he, she,* or *it.* When the subject is *I, you, we,* or *they,* the verb does not end in *s.*

Part A
Directions: Underline the correct verb form.

EXAMPLE

We (<u>work</u>, works) at the same company.

1. They (answer, answers) phones in the sales department.

2. She (file, files) invoices in the accounting department.

3. He (sort, sorts) letters in the mail room.

4. You (operate, operates) the computer.

5. I (help, helps) Tyrone with his orders.

6. He (buy, buys) new equipment and office supplies.

7. We (keep, keeps) careful records of all our purchases.

8. It (make, makes) us more efficient.

Part B
Directions: Underline and correct the five incorrect verbs.

EXAMPLE

     enjoy
We <u>enjoys</u> going to the club in my neighborhood.

It feature different bands every night. They plays my favorite music. You likes listening to music too. I wants you to go with me on Saturday. A woman will be singing popular songs. She sound great.

Check your answers on page 70.

Subject-Verb Agreement with Irregular Verbs _____

The verbs *be*, *do*, and *have* are ***irregular***.

Subject	Be	Do	Have
I	am, was	do	have
you	are, were	do	have
he, she, it	is, was	does	has
we, you, they	are, were	do	have

Directions: Underline the correct form of the irregular verb.

EXAMPLE

They (<u>have</u>, has) goals for the future.

1. He (have, has) a new job.

2. She (are, is) glad about returning to school.

3. She (do, does) her homework every night.

4. I (am, is) sure you will get good grades.

5. We (have, has) an excellent teacher.

6. He (do, does) everything to help the students.

7. They (are, is) eager to improve their skills.

8. I (do, does) much better on tests now.

9. You (were, was) the only person who could make a budget.

10. It (were, was) always hard for me to manage my money.

11. You (have, has) a list of bills to pay each month.

12. We (are, is) sometimes late in paying our bills.

13. I (have, has) tried to do better.

14. It (do, does) help to make a budget.

Check your answers on page 70.

Singular and Plural Nouns as Subjects

Present tense verbs end in *s* when the subject is *he, she, it,* or a singular noun. They do not end in *s* when the subject is *I, you, we, they,* or a plural noun. Singular subjects can be replaced by *he, she,* or *it.* Plural subjects can be replaced by *they.*

The <u>pitcher</u> (he) <u>throws</u> a ball.
The <u>fans</u> (they) <u>cheer</u> for the team.

Directions: Replace each subject with the correct pronoun. Then underline the correct verb form.

EXAMPLE　　　　The year (it) (are, <u>is</u>) 1955.

 1. An African-American woman named Rosa Parks (　　) (are, is) tired.

 2. Rosa Parks (　　) (board, boards) a bus in Montgomery, Alabama.

 3. Ms. Parks (　　) (sit, sits) near the front of the bus.

 4. The driver (　　) (order, orders) her to give her seat to a white man.

 5. Ms. Parks (　　) (do, does) not want to move.

 6. Ms. Parks (　　) (refuse, refuses) to obey the driver.

 7. The driver (　　) (swear, swears) at her.

 8. Then police officers (　　) (arrest, arrests) her.

 9. Friends (　　) (post, posts) bond to release her from jail.

10. African-American ministers (　　) (tell, tells) their congregations about Rosa Parks.

11. African-Americans (　　) (stop, stops) riding the buses.

12. Dr. Martin Luther King, Jr., (　　) (become, becomes) a leader of the protest.

13. The protest (　　) (are, is) an important event in the civil rights movement.

14. In 1956, the Supreme Court (　　) (say, says) that buses cannot be segregated.

Check your answers on page 70.

Compound Subjects Joined by *And*, *Or*, or *Nor* _____

Compound subjects have two parts. The two parts are always connected by *and, or,* or *nor.* Compound subjects joined by *and* are plural. They need a verb that agrees with a plural subject. When a compound subject is joined by *or* or *nor,* the verb agrees with the subject that is closer to the verb.

Part A
Directions: Underline the correct verb form.

EXAMPLE   Neither Theresa nor her friends (<u>like</u>, likes) sports.

1. Larry and Tina (are, is) baseball fans.

2. Either Larry or Tina (buy, buys) season tickets.

3. The Cubs and the Mets (are, is) their favorite teams.

4. Either Dwight Gooden or David Cone (pitch, pitches) today.

5. You and I (want, wants) to see the game on a big-screen TV.

6. Either Mark or his sons (collect, collects) baseball cards.

7. Cynthia and Gregory (read, reads) books about baseball.

8. Neither you nor I (enjoy, enjoys) hockey.

Part B
Directions: Complete each of the following sentences. Make sure that the verb you use agrees with the subject.

EXAMPLE   Gus or Milos *is in charge when I am away.*

1. Either Fran or her sisters _____

2. Neither the man nor his son _____

3. The doctor and the nurse _____

4. Saturday or Sunday _____

5. You and I _____

Check your answers on pages 70–71.

Subject-Verb Agreement with Describing Phrases ___

In many sentences, ***describing phrases*** come between the subject and verb.

The <u>stars</u> in the sky <u>shine</u> brightly.

Stars, the subject, is plural. *Shine*, the verb, agrees with the plural subject. The describing phrase, *in the sky*, does not affect subject-verb agreement.

Part A
Directions: Draw a line through the describing phrase in each sentence. Then underline the correct verb form.

EXAMPLE

Diets ~~around the world~~ (<u>differ</u>, differs).

1. People in China (have, has) rice as their main food.

2. Families from Turkey (enjoy, enjoys) yogurt.

3. A popular dish among many Middle Eastern people (are, is) pita bread with mashed chick-peas.

4. Many people in Africa (like, likes) red pepper sauce.

5. Lamb in cucumber sauce (are, is) popular in Greece.

Part B
Directions: This is a review of the subject-verb agreement rules you have learned. Underline the correct verb form in each sentence.

1. The parts of an animal's body (serve, serves) a purpose.

2. The fur on animals (keep, keeps) them warm.

3. Both the toad and the frog (catch, catches) insects with their sticky tongues.

4. A poisonous snake (have, has) sharp, deadly fangs.

5. Claws or toenails (help, helps) animals catch food.

Check your answers on page 71.

Commas

Commas have many uses. They can be used to interrupt a sentence with additional information, to connect or transition ideas, or to address a person directly.

1. **Additional Information**
   Maria Tallchief, a Native American, was a famous ballerina.
   I was born in Budapest, the capital city of Hungary.

2. **Connect or Transition Ideas**
   I am, of course, concerned about social problems.
   For example, the number of homeless people is growing.

3. **Direct Address**
   Nadia, when are you planning to move?
   Thank you, Sergio, for all your help.

Directions: Punctuate the interrupter in each sentence.

EXAMPLE Sarah, do you know who Luis Valdez is?

Valdez a writer and director is a very talented man. He helped start Teatro Campesino a Mexican-American theater group. It put on many plays about migrant farm workers people whom Valdez knew well. He is in fact the son of migrant farm workers.

In 1978, Valdez received a Rockefeller Foundation Award for writing *Zoot Suit* a play. Did you see the movie version Sarah? In my opinion it is a very good film.

In 1987, he directed *La Bamba* a movie about Ritchie Valens. Valens a 1950s rock star was also a migrant farm worker.

Check your answers on page 71.

WRITING ASSIGNMENT

AN EVENT IN YOUR LIFE

Directions: On another piece of paper, write a three-paragraph story about an event in your life. In the first paragraph, tell what happened before the event. In the second, tell what happened during the event. In the third, tell what happened after the event. Here are some suggestions for topics.

- ✪ The first time I ever baby-sat

- ✪ The time I bought my first car

- ✪ A time I overcame a fear

- ✪ A time I helped a friend in need

- ✪ The first time I ever drove a car

- ✪ The day I learned an important lesson

You can choose a different topic to write about. Just be sure to pick a topic that really interests you. When you are finished writing, use the Writing Checklist to look over what you wrote.

☑ WRITING CHECKLIST

- ☐ Is each of your three paragraphs indented?

- ☐ Do you have commas in the right places?

- ☐ Do your subjects and verbs agree?

ADJECTIVES AND ADVERBS

TEXT PAGES
120–124

Identifying Adjectives

Adjectives describe nouns by telling which one, what kind, or how many. Often an adjective comes directly before the noun it describes. However, an adjective can also come after the noun it describes.

Adjective before the noun: He is a <u>tall</u> **man**.

Adjective after the noun: The **man** is <u>tall</u>.

Directions: Draw two lines under the adjective that describes the underlined noun.

EXAMPLE

The Wizard of Oz is a <u>wonderful</u> <u>movie</u>.

1. Dorothy goes to a strange <u>land</u> called Oz.

2. She takes her little <u>dog</u> with her.

3. In Oz, Dorothy becomes friends with three <u>characters</u>.

4. Dorothy, the scarecrow, the tin man, and the cowardly lion all talk to a powerful <u>wizard</u>.

5. These <u>characters</u> want the wizard to grant their wishes.

6. They also meet a wicked <u>witch</u>.

7. The <u>witch</u> is cruel and sets the scarecrow on fire.

8. <u>Dorothy</u> is brave and kills the witch.

9. The <u>people</u> are glad and celebrate.

10. Dorothy's journey was really an incredible <u>dream</u>.

11. Many <u>people</u> enjoy watching *The Wizard of Oz.*

Check your answers on page 71.

Identifying Adverbs

Adverbs describe verbs by telling how, when, or where. Often an adverb comes directly after the verb it describes. However, an adverb can also come elsewhere in a sentence.

Adverb after the verb: The bus **appeared** <u>suddenly</u>.

Adverb elsewhere in the sentence: <u>Suddenly</u> the bus **appeared**.

Directions: Draw two lines under the adverb that describes the underlined verb.

EXAMPLE

In the early 1800s, America <u>was growing</u> quickly.

1. Women <u>were treated</u> unfairly during this time.

2. They <u>were</u> legally <u>denied</u> the right to vote for president.

3. Husbands still <u>controlled</u> their wives' property and money.

4. Some women unhappily <u>accepted</u> their role.

5. Susan B. Anthony <u>spoke</u> bravely on behalf of women's rights.

6. She honestly <u>felt</u> that women deserved more power.

7. She also thought that slaves <u>should be freed</u> immediately.

8. She <u>traveled</u> everywhere to talk about her opinions.

9. Susan B. Anthony often <u>visited</u> people in their homes.

10. Angrily she <u>protested</u> unfair laws for women.

11. Once someone <u>threw</u> acid at her during a speech.

12. Some political cartoons cruelly <u>showed</u> her as a bad person.

13. She never <u>quit</u> fighting for her cause.

14. Susan B. Anthony always <u>believed</u> in equality for women.

15. Finally in 1920, women <u>were given</u> the right to vote.

16. People today <u>respect</u> Susan B. Anthony's courage.

Check your answers on page 71.

Choosing Adjectives or Adverbs

If you want to describe a noun, use an adjective. If you want to describe a verb, use an adverb.

Adjective: The <u>strong</u> **wind** blew and knocked down telephone lines.

Adverb: The wind **blew** <u>strongly</u> and knocked down telephone lines.

Part A
Directions: Underline the correct form, adjective or adverb.

EXAMPLE Carla was sitting (quiet, <u>quietly</u>) in her apartment.

1. She heard her cups and plates rattle (noisy, noisily).

2. Her dresser began creeping (slow, slowly) across the room.

3. A (sudden, suddenly) earthquake had hit the city.

4. The walls of Carla's building shook (slight, slightly).

5. She heard (loud, loudly) sirens screech outside.

6. Carla (quick, quickly) packed some of her belongings.

7. She wanted to escape to a (safe, safely) place.

8. The city streets were (dangerous, dangerously).

9. (Terrible, terribly) fires were destroying a shopping mall.

Part B
Directions: Underline and correct the adjective or adverb error in each sentence.

gracefully
The figure skater moved <u>graceful</u> across the ice.

EXAMPLE

People cheered loud as she spun around. The skater was confidently.

Suddenly she jumped highly in the air. She landed easy. Her beautifully

costume sparkled under the lights. At the end of her act, she bowed and

skated quick to the sidelines.

Check your answers on pages 71–72.

Using Commas in a Series

A *series* consists of three or more similar items in a row. Commas are used after every item except the last one in a series.

Billie Holiday sang **powerful, sad,** and **beautiful** songs.
Joe plays **baseball, basketball,** and **football.**

Part A
Directions: Add commas to the sentences wherever needed. Some sentences may not need any commas.

EXAMPLE

Dan, Julie, and Sharon went to a Fourth of July celebration.

They saw fantastic exciting and incredible fireworks. Fireworks exploded banged and flashed in the sky. They looked so beautiful and bright. Everyone applauded as the fireworks boomed loudly and hissed faintly. After the show, Dan Julie and Sharon were hungry. They bought and ate hot dogs potato chips and lemonade.

Part B
Directions: Write sentences containing the series described below. Make sure you have at least three items separated by commas in each sentence.

1. Write a sentence about three cars you would like to own.

   _____

2. Write a sentence using three adjectives to describe a car.

   _____

3. Write a sentence using three adverbs to describe how a car rides.

   _____

Check your answers on page 72.

Punctuating Letters

Follow these rules to punctuate the parts of a letter.

1. Put a comma between the day of the month and the year.
May 4, 1994

2. Put a comma between the name of a city and a state.
Boston, MA 90017

3. Put a *comma* after the greeting of a *personal* letter.
Dear Lee,

4. Put a *colon* after the greeting of a *business* letter.
Dear Mr. Hernandez:

5. Put a comma after the closing of all letters.
Sincerely yours,

Directions: Add the missing punctuation to this business letter.

3102 North Riverview Road
Chicago IL 60657
July 2 199__

Ms. Jean Hall
Laramie Publishing Company
202 North Truman Road
Chicago IL 60601

Dear Ms. Hall

Please send me a copy of *Careers in the Food Industry*. I have enclosed a check for $6.50.

Sincerely

Lisa Byrd

Lisa Byrd

Check your answers on page 72.

W R I T I N G   A S S I G N M E N T

WRITING LETTERS

Part A: The Business Letter

Directions: Find the name and address of a travel agency in the yellow pages of the phone book. On another piece of paper, write a short business letter asking for information about a vacation. Ask about plane or train fares, hotel rates, and so on. Be sure to include all the parts of a business letter. When you are finished writing, use the Writing Checklist to look over what you wrote.

Part B: The Personal Letter

Directions: On another piece of paper, write a letter to a friend. Describe an experience you would like to share with that person. Use details that will help the person picture the experience. Include at least one series of items. Here are some suggestions for topics.

- ✪ A special friendship

- ✪ A job experience

- ✪ A change in your life

You can choose a different topic to write about. Just be sure to pick a topic that really interests you. When you are finished writing, use the Writing Checklist to look over what you wrote.

☑ W R I T I N G   C H E C K L I S T

☐ Does your personal letter have a date, a greeting, a body, a closing, and a signature?

☐ Does your business letter have a return address, a date, an inside address, a greeting, a body, a closing, and a signature?

☐ Is the punctuation correct?

COMBINING SENTENCES

TEXT PAGES
146–150 ## Using Conjunctions to Combine Sentences _____

Conjunctions are joining words. Seven common conjunctions are *and, but, yet, so, for, or,* and *nor.* Use a comma before a conjunction when it joins two complete sentences.

Directions: Underline the conjunction in each sentence, and add a comma in the correct place.

EXAMPLE

People admire Jackie Robinson, _for_ he was the first African-American to play on a major league baseball team.

His family did not have a lot of money yet he was still able to fulfill his dreams. Jackie Robinson went to Pasadena Junior College and then he went to the University of California at Los Angeles. Robinson played many different sports in college and he excelled in all of them. He had money problems during his junior year so he had to drop out of college.

Robinson was a soldier during World War II and then he joined an all-black baseball team called the Kansas City Monarchs. Branch Rickey was the president of the Brooklyn Dodgers and he saw Robinson play. Rickey realized Robinson was a great player so he asked him to join the Brooklyn farm team. Robinson had an outstanding batting average so he was brought up to play for the Brooklyn Dodgers in 1947.

Racist fans sometimes booed Jackie Robinson but he didn't let racism stop him. He later became active in the civil rights movement for he believed in equality and freedom.

Check your answers on page 72.

Using Connectors

Connectors are another kind of joining word used to combine sentences. Some common connectors are *however, moreover, therefore,* and *instead.* When a connector joins two complete sentences, put a semicolon (;) before the connector and a comma (,) after it.

Directions: Use one of the connectors listed above to combine each pair of sentences. Be sure to add the correct punctuation.

EXAMPLE

Bart has gained weight. He has decided to go on a diet.

Bart has gained weight; therefore, he has decided to go on a diet.

1. Dr. Sanders told Bart to eat foods low in fat. He said that Bart should avoid salty foods.

_____

_____

2. Bart used to eat fried foods. He now eats foods that are broiled or baked.

_____

_____

3. Bart doesn't like to exercise. He knows that working out will help him lose weight more quickly.

_____

_____

4. Bart walks a mile each day. He goes to the gym once a week and uses the exercise machines.

_____

_____

5. Bart is motivated. He will probably stick to his diet and exercise plan.

_____

_____

Check your answers on page 72.

Using Subordinating Conjunctions

Subordinating conjunctions are used to join two parts of the same sentence. The part that begins with the subordinating conjunction is called the *subordinate clause*. Some common subordinating conjunctions are *because, although, if, when, before, after.* Put a comma after a subordinate clause when it begins a sentence. Do not punctuate when the clause is at the end of the sentence.

If you have any questions, please give me a call.
Please give me a call **if you have any questions.**

Directions: Use one of the subordinating conjunctions listed above to combine the two parts of each sentence. Be sure to add a comma when needed.

EXAMPLE

Felicia has a baby-sitter ___because___ she works full-time.

1. _____ she is a single parent she needs to earn more money to support her child.

2. Felicia brings her son, Will, to the baby-sitter's house _____ she goes to work.

3. _____ Felicia leaves the baby-sitter takes Will to the playground.

4. _____ Felicia likes her job she would rather stay home with Will.

5. Sometimes Felicia has to miss a day of work _____ Will is sick.

6. Felicia will no longer need a baby-sitter _____ her company opens a day-care center.

7. _____ she likes the sitter Felicia is looking forward to the center's opening.

8. Felicia is excited _____ she will have more time with her son.

Check your answers on page 73.

WRITING ASSIGNMENT

WRITING A PARAGRAPH

Directions: On another piece of paper, write a paragraph describing a person, place, or thing. Use eight short sentences. Then combine some of the sentences using connectors, conjunctions, and subordinating conjunctions. Here are some suggestions for topics.

- ✪ Your ideal mate
- ✪ Your ideal boss
- ✪ Your favorite vacation spot
- ✪ A room in your home
- ✪ A pet
- ✪ A gift that you treasure

You can choose a different topic to write about. Just be sure to pick a topic that really interests you. When you are finished writing, use the Writing Checklist to look over what you wrote.

☑ WRITING CHECKLIST

- ☐ Do you have at least eight sentences in your paragraph?
- ☐ Have you used sentence-combining techniques correctly?
- ☐ Did you punctuate your sentences correctly?

NEW TOPICS IN SENTENCE STRUCTURE

TEXT PAGES
167–170

Identifying Misplaced Describing Phrases _____

A *describing phrase* gives information about a noun or a pronoun. Place a describing phrase next to the word it describes. Otherwise, the describing phrase is misplaced.

Misplaced: Flashing across the sky, we saw **lightning**.
The phrase *flashing across the sky* should be next to *lightning*.

Correctly placed: We saw **lightning** flashing across the sky.

Directions: Put a check mark next to the correctly written sentence in each pair.

___

EXAMPLE

✓   Families on budgets can reduce their food bills.

_____   Families can reduce their food bills on budgets.

_____ **1.** Shopping at discount markets, Esta saves money on groceries.

_____   Esta saves money on groceries shopping at discount markets.

_____ **2.** These markets are popular in many cities and suburbs, also called superstores.

_____   These markets, also called superstores, are popular in many cities and suburbs.

_____ **3.** Esta reaches for cans stacked high on the shelves.

_____   Stacked high on the shelves, Esta reaches for cans.

_____ **4.** Esta gives coupons from the Sunday paper to the cashier.

_____   Esta gives coupons to the cashier from the Sunday paper.

Check your answers on page 73.

Parallel Structure

Parallel structure means that items in a sentence are in the same form.

Not parallel: Al's jobs are <u>cleaning floors</u> and <u>to wash windows.</u>

Parallel: Al's jobs are <u>cleaning floors</u> and <u>washing windows.</u>

Directions: Put a check mark next to the sentence that correctly uses parallel structure.

EXAMPLE _____   Rafael thinks that big cities are dirty, crowded, and have danger.

✓   Rafael thinks that big cities are dirty, crowded, and dangerous.

_____ **1.** Moving to the suburbs and to buy a home are Rafael's future plans.

_____   Moving to the suburbs and buying a home are Rafael's future plans.

_____ **2.** He wants his children to play in safer parks and going to better schools.

_____   He wants his children to play in safer parks and to go to better schools.

_____ **3.** The mayor has not succeeded in improving education or lowering the crime rate.

_____   The mayor has not succeeded in improving education or to lower the crime rate.

_____ **4.** Rafael believes that the city government is weak, dishonest, and doesn't care.

_____   Rafael believes that the city government is weak, dishonest, and uncaring.

Check your answers on page 73.

Paragraph Structure _____

A *topic sentence* expresses the main idea of a paragraph. The *supporting sentences* give details that explain the topic sentence.

Directions: For each paragraph, underline the topic sentence. Then draw a line through the sentence that does not support the topic sentence.

EXAMPLE

For several reasons, autumn is my favorite time of year. I enjoy the crisp fall weather. I love watching the leaves turn to gold, red, and orange. My kids get excited about going back to school and seeing their classmates again. Autumn also brings the return of football. ~~Baseball is the most popular sport in the United States, but football is almost as popular.~~

1. Cities in the United States grew for different reasons. Pittsburgh developed because of its iron and steel industry. Automobile factories led to Detroit's growth. The movie business helped make Los Angeles a major city. Many people like to visit Hollywood and search for their favorite movie stars. Because of nightclubs and gambling, Las Vegas became a center of entertainment.

2. Helicopters have many uses. Flying overhead in helicopters, forest rangers watch for forest fires. Helicopters help cowboys round up cattle. During wars, helicopters carry soldiers into enemy territory and rescue wounded soldiers. Soldiers who fought in these wars were very brave. News shows rely on helicopters for the daily traffic reports.

3. New laws are helping single parents collect child support. One of these laws is the Family Support Act of 1988. This law helps divorced mothers and fathers. Divorces are more common now than they were a hundred years ago. Suppose that a father refuses to pay child support. The court can order his employer to set aside money from each paycheck. Then a government agency sends the money to the mother.

Check your answers on page 73.

WRITING ASSIGNMENT

THREE PARAGRAPHS

Part A: Descriptive Paragraph

Directions: On another piece of paper, write a paragraph describing a beautiful place. Use adjectives to create an interesting word picture. Include the sights, sounds, or smells of the place. When you are finished writing, use the Writing Checklist to look over what you wrote.

Part B: Story Paragraph

Directions: On another piece of paper, write a paragraph about something interesting that happened to you. First, tell what led up to the incident. Second, tell what happened during the incident. Finally, tell what happened after the incident. When you are finished writing, use the Writing Checklist to look over what you wrote.

Part C: Opinion Paragraph

Directions: On another piece of paper, write your opinion of a movie you recently saw. Explain why you thought the movie was either good or bad. Give reasons and examples to support your opinion. When you are finished writing, use the Writing Checklist to look over what you wrote.

☑ WRITING CHECKLIST

- ☐ Does each paragraph have a topic sentence?

- ☐ Have you used colorful adjectives in your descriptive paragraph?

- ☐ Does your story paragraph tell what happened in time order?

- ☐ Did you use reasons and examples in your opinion paragraph?

POST-TEST

This Post-Test will give you a chance to see how much you remember about what you have studied. Take the test without looking in the book for help or answers.

The Post-Test has been divided into two sections. The first section is a test of your overall knowledge of language skills. The second section is a test of your writing ability and asks you to write a paragraph.

Once you complete the test, check your answers on pages 61–62. Then fill out the Post-Test Evaluation Chart on page 63. This chart will tell you which sections of the book you might want to review.

Section I

Part A: Nouns and Pronouns

This part tests your knowledge of common and proper nouns, singular and plural nouns, and possessive nouns. It also tests your knowledge of subject, object, and possessive pronouns.

Directions: Each of the following sentences has an underlined part. Below each sentence are three options for writing the underlined part. Circle the number of the option that makes the sentence correct. The first option is always the same as the underlined part of the original sentence.

EXAMPLE

After the Civil War, <u>many childs worked in factorys</u>.

(1) many childs worked in factorys

(2) many children worked in factories

(3) many children worked in factorys

1. <u>They're familys</u> needed the extra money.

   (1) They're familys

   (2) Their families

   (3) There families

2. Working conditions were also bad for <u>man and woman</u>.

   (1) man and woman

   (2) men and women

   (3) mens and womens

3. Bosses gave <u>them</u> low salaries.

    (1) them

    (2) they

    (3) him

4. Many <u>americans</u> worked 60 to 70 hours a week.

    (1) americans

    (2) Americans'

    (3) Americans

5. Working <u>peoples'</u> lives were in danger because of unsafe machines.

    (1) peoples'

    (2) people's

    (3) peoples

6. Most bosses didn't listen to <u>employee's</u> complaints.

    (1) employee's

    (2) employees

    (3) employees'

7. Today, a factory <u>workers'</u> life is much better.

    (1) workers'

    (2) worker's

    (3) workers

8. Raymond, a welder, tells you and <u>I about he's job</u>.

    (1) I about he's job

    (2) me about his job

    (3) I about his job

9. <u>He</u> gets health insurance and overtime pay.

    (1) He

    (2) Him

    (3) His

10. He belongs to a <u>Labor Union called the united auto workers</u>.

    (1) Labor Union called the united auto workers

    (2) labor Union called the United Auto workers

    (3) labor union called the United Auto Workers

Part B: Verbs

This part tests your knowledge of verb tenses, irregular verb forms, and subject-verb agreement.

Directions: Underline the correct form of the verb to complete each sentence.

EXAMPLE   Next week, two candidates for the school board (<u>will give</u>, gave) speeches.

1. Brenda Jones and Gloria Ramirez (believe, believes) in improving education.

2. Both women (are, is) against lowering teachers' salaries.

3. Neither you nor I (want, wants) another teachers' strike.

4. Today we (were discussing, was discussing) which candidate is better.

5. Jones (work, works) at a local hospital.

6. Last year, Ramirez (graduates, graduated) from law school.

7. They both (do, does) volunteer work in the community.

8. The children in the school (need, needs) more special programs and activities.

9. The average size of the classes (are, is) 40 students.

10. Last week, a gang (sells, sold) drugs on the playground.

11. Either Jones or Ramirez (have, has) to deal with these important problems.

12. Ramirez really (understand, understands) the parents' point of view.

13. Yesterday, she (writes, wrote) a letter to the editor of the newspaper.

14. It (were, was) about changing the public school system.

Part C: Sentence Structure

This part tests your knowledge of different methods of combining ideas in sentences—using joining words, describing phrases, and parallel construction.

Directions: Each of the following sentences has an underlined part. Below each sentence are three options for writing the underlined part. Circle the number of the option that makes the sentence correct. The first option is always the same as the underlined part of the original sentence.

EXAMPLE

The tap dancers shuffled, turned, and they jumped.

(1) they jumped

(2) jumped

(3) they were jumping

1. The company was losing money or it laid off workers.

   (1) money or

   (2) money, or

   (3) money, so

2. Wearing a ski mask, the police chased the robber.

   (1) Wearing a ski mask, the police chased the robber.

   (2) The police chased the robber wearing a ski mask.

   (3) The police wearing a ski mask chased the robber.

3. Mothers in TV shows of the 1950s stayed at home, therefore, mothers in today's TV shows have jobs.

   (1) home, therefore, mothers

   (2) home; therefore, mothers

   (3) home; however, mothers

4. After the war ended the city honored the returning soldiers.

   (1) ended the

   (2) ended, the

   (3) ended; the

5. The woman was going to an interview on the bus.

   (1) The woman was going to an interview on the bus.

   (2) On the bus, the woman was going to an interview.

   (3) The woman on the bus was going to an interview.

6. Lester forgot to punch the time clock before he left work.

   (1) clock before

   (2) clock, before

   (3) clock; before

7. Jim spoke quickly, excitedly, and in a nervous manner.

   (1) in a nervous manner

   (2) nervously

   (3) nervous

8. The quarterback threw a good pass, so the receiver missed it.

   (1) pass, so

   (2) pass, but

   (3) pass, or

9. The man on the game show solved the puzzle; however, he won the grand prize.

   (1) puzzle; however,

   (2) puzzle; instead,

   (3) puzzle; therefore,

10. Laws can give people more freedom, yet they can also take away certain rights.

   (1) freedom, yet

   (2) freedom, nor

   (3) freedom, because

11. Because Sylvia learned to use the computer; she got a new job.

   (1) computer; she

   (2) computer, she

   (3) computer she

Part D: Punctuation

This part tests your knowledge of the punctuation marks you have studied.

Directions: Only one of the sentences in each of the following groups is punctuated correctly. Circle the number of the correct sentence.

EXAMPLE

(1) The telephone, the telegraph and the phonograph were all invented in the 1800s.

(2) The telephone, the telegraph, and the phonograph were all invented during the 1800s.

(3) The telephone, the telegraph, and the phonograph, were all invented during the 1800s.

1. (1) Alexander Graham Bell, a speech teacher invented the telephone.

(2) Alexander Graham Bell a speech teacher, invented the telephone.

(3) Alexander Graham Bell, a speech teacher, invented the telephone.

2. (1) In fact, did you know that Bell sent the first message over the phone in 1876.

(2) In fact did you know that Bell sent the first message over the phone in 1876!

(3) In fact, did you know that Bell sent the first message over the phone in 1876?

3. (1) Bell said, "Mr. Watson, come here."

(2) Bell said, "Mr. Watson come here?

(3) Bell said, "Mr. Watson come here.

4. (1) Thomas A. Watson Bell's assistant, helped him test this wonderful machine.

(2) Thomas A. Watson, Bell's assistant helped him test this wonderful machine.

(3) Thomas A. Watson, Bell's assistant, helped him test this wonderful machine.

5. (1) The telephone was'nt available to the public until 1878.

    (2) The telephone wasn't available to the public until 1878.

    (3) The telephone wasnt available to the public until 1878.

6. (1) Can you imagine not having a telephone?

    (2) Can you imagine not having a telephone!

    (3) Can you imagine not having a telephone.

7. (1) Doctors, police, and fire fighters appreciate its importance in saving lives.

    (2) Doctors, police and fire fighters appreciate it's importance in saving lives.

    (3) Doctors, police and fire fighters appreciate its' importance in saving lives.

8. (1) The telephone is of course crucial to businesses.

    (2) The telephone is, of course, crucial to businesses.

    (3) The telephone is, of course crucial to businesses.

9. (1) How much does youre family rely on it.

    (2) How much does you're family rely on it!

    (3) How much does your family rely on it?

Section II

Writing a Paragraph

Directions: This section of the test will give you a chance to demonstrate how well you write. Pick just one of the three suggested topics. Read the choices carefully. You should brainstorm or cluster ideas before you begin writing. When you finish writing, use the Writing Checklist to look over what you wrote.

Topic 1

Imagine what your perfect vacation would be like. Where would you go? What would you do? In a paragraph, describe your perfect vacation. Include vivid details that create a word picture of the place.

Topic 2

Think of a person who has influenced your life. Perhaps a close friend, a relative, or a teacher gave you good advice or helped you solve a problem. In a paragraph, explain how this person influenced you. What did he or she do?

Topic 3

Think of a situation in which you had a conflict with someone. For example, maybe you disagreed with a co-worker or argued with a friend. Write a paragraph telling the story of the conflict. Be sure to explain the reason for the conflict.

☑ W R I T I N G   C H E C K L I S T

☐ Have you used the information you have learned about writing and organizing paragraphs?

☐ Did you check spelling, capitalization, punctuation, and sentence structure?

POST-TEST ANSWER KEY

SECTION I

Part A: Nouns and Pronouns
1. **(2)** The possessive form *their* is correct because it refers to children. *Families* should end in *ies*.

2. **(2)** The correct plural forms of *man* and *woman* are *men* and *women*.

3. **(1)** The object pronoun *them* is correct because it is not the subject of the sentence. The pronoun must be plural because it refers to *men and women*.

4. **(3)** The noun *Americans* is capitalized because it names a specific group of people.

5. **(2)** When a plural noun does not end in *s*, add an *'s* to make it possessive.

6. **(3)** Add an apostrophe to a plural noun ending in *s* to show possession.

7. **(2)** Add an *'s* to a singular noun to show possession.

8. **(2)** The object pronoun *me* is correct because it is not the subject of the sentence. The possessive form *his* is correct because it refers to *Raymond*.

9. **(1)** *He* is the correct form because it is a subject pronoun.

10. **(3)** The words *labor union* are not capitalized because they do not name a specific organization. *United Auto Workers* is capitalized because it names a specific union.

Part B: Verbs
1. **(believe)** Two subjects joined by *and* are plural.

2. **(are)** The verb agrees with the plural subject *women*.

3. **(want)** The two subjects are joined by *nor*. The verb agrees with the closer subject, *I*.

4. **(were discussing)** The verb form agrees with the plural subject *we*.

5. **(works)** The verb agrees with the singular subject *Jones*.

6. **(graduated)** The time clue *Last year* tells you to use the past tense.

7. **(do)** The verb form agrees with the plural subject *They*.

8. **(need)** The verb agrees with the plural subject *children*.

9. **(is)** The verb form agrees with the singular subject *size*.

10. **(sold)** The time clue *Last week* tells you to use the past tense.

11. **(has)** The two subjects are joined by *or*. The verb agrees with the closer subject, *Ramirez*.

12. **(understands)** The verb form agrees with the singular subject *Ramirez*.

13. **(wrote)** The time clue *Yesterday* tells you to use the past tense.

14. **(was)** The verb form agrees with the singular subject *It*.

Part C: Sentence Structure
1. **(3)** The conjunction *so* shows that the first part of the sentence caused the second part of the sentence. Note that a comma is used before the conjunction.

2. **(2)** The original sentence says that the police were wearing a ski mask. The describing phrase *wearing a ski mask* should be next to *robber*.

3. **(3)** The connector *however* shows that the second part of the sentence contrasts with the first part of the sentence. Note the correct punctuation for this joining word.

4. **(2)** A comma goes after a subordinate clause when it begins a sentence.

5. **(3)** The original sentence says that the interview was on the bus. The describing phrase *on the bus* should be next to *woman*.

6. (1) No punctuation is necessary because the subordinate clause follows the main part of the sentence.

7. (2) The items *quickly, excitedly,* and *nervously* are all parallel.

8. (2) The conjunction *but* shows a contrast between the two parts of the sentence. Note the correct punctuation for this joining word.

9. (3) The connector *therefore* shows that the first part of the sentence caused the second part of the sentence. Note the correct punctuation for this joining word.

10. (1) No correction is necessary because the conjunction *yet* shows a contrast.

11. (2) A comma goes after a subordinate clause when it begins a sentence.

Part D: Punctuation

1. (3) Set off the phrase giving additional information, *a speech teacher*, with commas.

2. (3) The sentence is a question. Set off the interrupting phrase, *In fact*, with a comma.

3. (1) The sentence contains a direct quotation that is a statement. Set off the direct address, *Mr. Watson*, with a comma.

4. (3) Set off the phrase giving additional information, *Bell's assistant*, with commas.

5. (2) The apostrophe takes the place of the missing letter *o* when the words *was not* are made into the contraction *wasn't*.

6. (1) The sentence is in the form of a question.

7. (1) Place commas after every item of a series except the last one. The possessive pronoun *its* refers to *telephone* and is not a contraction.

8. (2) Set off the interrupting phrase, *of course*, with commas.

9. (3) The sentence is a question. The possessive pronoun *your* is correct.

SECTION II

Writing a Paragraph

In this section of the post-test, you wrote a paragraph on your own. If possible, have an instructor work with you to evaluate your paragraph. If you are evaluating your paragraph on your own, be sure to put it aside for a day or two. Then use the following questions to look over your writing. Note that page numbers refer to *Pre-GED Writing and Language Skills*, the textbook that goes along with this workbook.

1. Does your paragraph have a clear topic sentence? Topic sentences are explained on pages 176–178.

2. Do other sentences in the paragraph support the topic sentence? Supporting sentences are discussed on pages 176–178.

3. Did you have trouble coming up with ideas to put in your paragraph? If so, review clustering on pages 24–25 and brainstorming on pages 96–97.

4. Did you have problems with verbs, pronouns, commas, or other areas of grammar? If so, you can find pages to review in the table of contents.

5. If you want to try writing another paragraph, go back to Section II of the post-test on page 60 of this workbook. Choose another topic to write about, and evaluate it in the same way. Remember that the best way to improve your writing is to write.

POST-TEST EVALUATION CHART

On the chart, find the number of each question you missed on the Post-Test and circle it. Then you will know what pages of the main textbook to review before you move on to Contemporary's *GED Test 1: Writing Skills* book.

Language Skills	Item Numbers	Review Pages	Number Correct
Part A: Nouns and Pronouns			
Nouns	1, 2, 4, 5, 6, 7, 10	45–55	
Pronouns	1, 3, 8, 9	45, 55–65	_____/10
Part B: Verbs			
Verb tense	6, 10, 13	70–88	
Subject-verb agreement	1, 2, 3, 4, 5, 7, 8, 9, 11, 12, 14	98–115	_____/14
Part C: Sentence Structure			
Conjunctions	1, 8, 10	146–150	
Connectors	3, 9	151–155	
Subordinating conjunctions	4, 6, 11	156–160	
Describing phrases	2, 5	167–171	
Parallel structure	7	171–174	_____/11
Part D: Punctuation			
Quotation marks	3	88–90	
Types of sentences	2, 3, 6, 9	29–31	
Contractions	5	62–65	
Interrupters	1, 2, 4, 8	110–115	
Series commas	7	131–133	_____/9
		Total Correct	_____/44

ANSWER KEY

PARTS OF SPEECH

Nouns
Page 2
Part A

1. Lenora, trumpet, saxophone, clarinet

2. Jack, piano, organ, guitar

3. Jack, Lenora, band, friends

4. band, clubs, Chicago, Detroit

5. sister, brother, money, musicians

6. parents, Jack, Lenora, school

7. dream, kids, education

8. fall, sister, brother, classes

Part B

Use these lists to check your work. It's OK if your nouns are different from these.

List 1	List 2	List 3
Michael Jordan	the moon	new house
the president	Disney World	Porsche
Mother Theresa	Hawaii	CD player

Pronouns
Page 3
Part A

1. you, her

2. She, them

3. Our, her

4. She, We

5. It

6. They, their

7. them

Part B

1. he

2. It, him

3. he

4. They

5. His

Verbs
Page 4
Part A

1. stole

2. pointed, took

3. raced

4. described

5. were, wore

6. searched

7. was

Part B

Use these sentences to check your work. It's OK if your sentences are different from these.

1. The ball <u>soars</u> through the air.

2. The wide receiver <u>jumps</u> into the air and <u>catches</u> it.

3. He <u>runs</u> toward the end zone.

4. He <u>makes</u> a touchdown!

5. The crowd <u>rises</u> to its feet and <u>cheers</u>.

Adjectives
Page 5
Part A

1. some, beautiful, sunny

2. clean, white

3. warm, fragrant

4. soothing, gentle

5. these, wonderful

Part B

Use these adjectives to check your work. It's OK if your adjectives are different from these.

1. loud

2. Romantic

3. Several

4. these

Adverbs
Page 6
Part A
1. neatly
2. carefully
3. quickly
4. there
5. Later

Part B
Use these adverbs to check your work. It's OK if your adverbs are different from these.
1. nervously
2. nearby
3. everywhere
4. Soon
5. cheerfully

WHAT IS A SENTENCE?

Identifying Sentences and Fragments
Page 8
Part A
1. S
2. S
3. F
4. S
5. F
6. F
7. S
8. F

Part B
1. Believing it to be wrong.
2. Started the *New York Times*.
3. Against the death penalty.
4. Nominated for president by the Liberal Republican party.

Turning Fragments into Sentences
Page 9
Use these sentences to check your work. It's OK if your sentences are different from these. Just be sure that your sentences are complete.
1. The interviewer described the job, salary, and benefits.
2. The person who was hired would be working on a computer.
3. The salary was $300 a week.
4. All full-time employees receive group health insurance.
5. The man was hired for the job.
6. He felt happy because he liked working on the computer.

Types of Sentences
Page 10
Part A
1. ? / question
2. . / command
3. . / statement
4. . / statement *or* ! / exclamation
5. . / command

Part B
Use these sentences to check your work. It's OK if your sentences are different from these. Just be sure that you used the correct endmarks.
1. How do you fix a leaky faucet?
2. The horror movie gave me terrible nightmares!
3. The new restaurant serves delicious tacos.
4. Do not drive a car if you have been drinking.

Mistakes in Sentences
Page 11

Use this paragraph to check your work. It's OK if your sentences are different from these. Just be sure that your sentences are complete.

Different cultures have different ideas about how and why people dream. People in some cultures believe there is a dream world. They think this world is a place where the soul goes when a person is asleep. These people believe that a person's soul may become lost in the dream world if he or she is suddenly awakened. As a result, they are careful not to disturb sleepers. People in other cultures believe that events in their dreams are real. These people have been known to end friendships after dreaming that their friends did them harm. In some cultures, dreams are believed to be clues to the future. People in these cultures may go to a medicine man or other religious leader for help in figuring out what a dream means.

Finding the Subject
Page 12
Part A

1. Machines help
2. tractor is
3. Plows are
4. blades loosen
5. Crops need
6. Fertilizers are
7. Farmers spread
8. insects ruin
9. locust eats
10. Scientists developed
11. pesticides were
12. People want

Part B

Use these sentences to check your work. It's OK if your sentences are different from these. Just be sure that you found the subject and verb in each.

1. Chefs chop vegetables in food processors.
2. Dairy farmers use milking machines.
3. Tailors mend clothing on sewing machines.

Finding Tricky Subjects
Page 13
Part A

1. diet
2. diet
3. you
4. labels
5. (You)
6. labels
7. you
8. (You)

Part B

Use these sentences to check your work. It's OK if your sentences are different from these. Just be sure that you used the correct endmark.

1. Eat plenty of fruits and vegetables.
2. What is the nutritional content of your food?
3. For breakfast, you should eat cereal with skimmed milk and fruit.

Action and Linking Predicates
Page 14
Part A

Use these action verbs to check your work. It's OK if your verbs are different from these. Just be sure that your verbs show action.

1. crawled
2. tried
3. went
4. wore
5. sipped

Part B

Use these sentences to check your work. It's OK if your sentences are different from these. Just be sure that you added a linking verb and an adjective to each sentence.

1. am tall
2. is patient
3. were beautiful
4. are violent
5. is interesting
6. was popular

NOUNS AND PRONOUNS

Capitalizing Proper Nouns
Page 16
Part A
1. Dallas
2. Elm Street
3. Dallas Parkland Hospital, Kennedy
4. Texas, John B. Connally
5. Kennedy, Arlington National Cemetery, Washington, D.C.
6. Americans
7. Christmas
8. *JFK*

Part B
Abraham Lincoln served as president during the Civil War. On April 14, 1865, he and his wife went to Ford's Theater to see a play. During the play, John Wilkes Booth shot and killed President Lincoln.

Forming Plural Nouns
Page 17
Part A
The Amish are a group with strong religious beliefs. They pray regularly in their churches. The Amish don't live in large cities. They live in small communities. The Amish live by strict rules. Amish women wear caps and shawls in public. The men wear hats most of the time. The children don't watch TV or talk on the phone. The Amish ride in horse-drawn buggies instead of cars.

Part B
1. boxes
2. factories
3. persons *or* people
4. attorneys
5. desks

Possessive Nouns
Page 18
Part A
1. carpenters' tools
2. a baby's bottle
3. a doctor's office
4. friends' advice
5. women's rights

Part B
They wanted the teachers' strike to end. Their children's education was at stake. Many students went to their friends' houses during the day. The school's bus drivers were also losing money.

Subject and Object Pronouns
Page 19
Part A
1. It
2. They
3. them
4. He
5. We
6. She
7. us
8. him
9. her
10. You

Part B
Use these sentences to check your work. It's OK if your sentences are different from these. Just be sure that you used pronouns correctly.
1. We love action pictures.
2. They are fun to watch.
3. My favorites have car chases in them.
4. Chases keep me on the edge of my seat.

Possessive Pronouns
Page 20
Part A
1. his
2. its
3. their
4. his
5. Mine
6. their
7. ours
8. yours

Part B
Use these sentences to check your work. It's OK if your sentences are different from these. Just be sure that you used pronouns correctly.
1. Do you like your job?
2. The responsibility is yours.
3. That computer is theirs.
4. The dog hurt its tail.
5. You can borrow mine.

Contractions and Possessive Pronouns
Page 21
Part A
1. They're
2. you're
3. he'll
4. doesn't
5. wouldn't
6. I'm
7. It's
8. That's
9. don't
10. We'll

Part B
Did they get their shots? My son is in your daughter's class. I know it's hard raising children by yourself. I've been a single parent for three years. Let's have lunch sometime.

VERBS: FORM AND TENSE

Choosing Present Tense Verbs
Page 23
1. doctor, listens
2. She, puts
3. heart, makes
4. heart, works
5. heart, pumps
6. hearts, weigh
7. Arteries, carry
8. They, resemble
9. Veins, move
10. Dr. Yung, takes
11. blood, looks
12. technicians, examine

Past and Future Tenses of Regular Verbs
Page 24
Part A
1. walked
2. planted
3. saluted
4. described
5. looked
6. watched
7. talked
8. enjoyed
9. jumped
10. stayed

Part B
1. roasted, will roast
2. baked, will bake
3. boiled, will boil
4. prepared, will prepare
5. mashed, will mash

Past Tense of Irregular Verbs
Page 25
Part A
1. became
2. won
3. led
4. found
5. stood
6. spoke
7. told
8. fought
9. felt
10. lost

Part B
He had season tickets. He usually took Molly with him. They bought hot dogs and sat in the upper deck. They got mad when their favorite players struck out.

Forms of *Be*
Page 26
Part A
1. are
2. is
3. was
4. were
5. were
6. was

7. are

8. are

9. was

Part B

We <u>were</u> watching a television show. A young man <u>was</u> interviewing other single men. A young woman <u>was</u> asking for their phone numbers. I <u>am</u> going to watch tomorrow's show. The guests <u>are</u> going to be soap opera stars.

Forms of *Have* and *Do*
Page 27
Part A

1. will have

2. has

3. has

4. have

5. had

6. had

7. has

Part B

1. do

2. did

3. did

4. will do

5. does

6. Do

7. did

Time Clues to Verb Tenses
Page 28
Part A

1. thought

2. know

3. allowed

4. ban

5. smoked

6. will attend

7. will take

8. will prohibit

Part B

Use these sentences to check your work. It's OK if your sentences are different from these. Just be sure that you used the correct verb tenses.

1. Today I have to work.

2. Yesterday I had the day off.

3. Last year I attended school.

4. Tomorrow I will finish this project.

The Continuing Tenses
Page 29
Part A

1. is

2. are

3. am

4. is

5. are

6. are

Part B

1. was

2. were

3. was

4. were

5. were

6. was

Using Quotation Marks
Page 30

1. "What was the article about?" John asked.

2. Arnie replied, "It's about children playing sports."

3. "My ten-year-old, Bobby, plays on a football team," John said.

4. "According to the article, he shouldn't," Arnie said.

5. John asked, "What are the reasons?"

6. Arnie answered, "His body isn't developed enough."

7. "But Bobby is big for his age!" John explained.

8. Arnie warned, "It's still risky because he could get injured."

9. John remarked, "A teammate of Bobby's did break a leg."

10. "Many athletes his age break bones," said Arnie.

11. Arnie added, "Some children put too much pressure on themselves."

12. "Bobby does get very upset when the team loses, " John admitted.

13. "Doctors think that young children should play sports just for the fun of it," Arnie said.

14. Arnie asked, "What do you think?"

15. "Maybe they're right," John replied.

SUBJECT-VERB AGREEMENT

Pronouns as Subjects
Page 32
Part A
1. answer

2. files

3. sorts

4. operate

5. help

6. buys

7. keep

8. makes

Part B
It features different bands every night. They play my favorite music. You like listening to music too. I want you to go with me on Saturday. A woman will be singing popular songs. She sounds great.

Subject-Verb Agreement with Irregular Verbs
Page 33
1. has

2. is

3. does

4. am

5. have

6. does

7. are

8. do

9. were

10. was

11. have

12. are

13. have

14. does

Singular and Plural Nouns as Subjects
Page 34
1. she, is

2. she, boards

3. she, sits

4. he (or she), orders

5. she, does

6. she, refuses

7. he (or she), swears

8. they, arrest

9. they, post

10. they, tell

11. they, stop

12. he, becomes

13. it, is

14. it, says

Compound Subjects Joined by *And*, *Or*, or *Nor*
Page 35
Part A
1. are

2. buys

3. are

4. pitches

5. want

6. collect

7. read

8. enjoy

Part B
Use these sentences to check your work. It's OK if your sentences are different from these. Just be that sure your verbs agree with the subjects.
1. Either Fran or her sisters work at the community center.

2. Neither the man nor his son <u>has a job</u>.

3. The doctor and the nurse <u>help patients in the hospital</u>.

4. Saturday or Sunday <u>is a good day to go</u>.

5. You and I <u>always have a good time</u>.

Subject-Verb Agreement with Describing Phrases
Page 36
Part A
1. in China, have

2. from Turkey, enjoy

3. among many Middle Eastern people, is

4. in Africa, like

5. in cucumber sauce, is

Part B
1. serve

2. keeps

3. catch

4. has

5. help

Commas
Page 37
Valdez, a writer and director, is a very talented man. He helped start Teatro Campesino, a Mexican-American theater group. It put on many plays about migrant farm workers, people whom Valdez knew well. He is, in fact, the son of migrant farm workers.

In 1978, Valdez received a Rockefeller Foundation Award for writing *Zoot Suit*, a play. Did you see the movie version, Sarah? In my opinion, it is a very good film.

In 1987, he directed *La Bamba*, a movie about Ritchie Valens. Valens, a 1950s rock star, was also a migrant farm worker.

ADJECTIVES AND ADVERBS

Identifying Adjectives
Page 39
1. strange

2. little

3. three

4. powerful

5. These

6. wicked

7. cruel

8. brave

9. glad

10. incredible

11. Many

Identifying Adverbs
Page 40
1. unfairly

2. legally

3. still

4. unhappily

5. bravely

6. honestly

7. immediately

8. everywhere

9. often

10. Angrily

11. Once

12. cruelly

13. never

14. always

15. Finally

16. today

Choosing Adjectives or Adverbs
Page 41
Part A
1. noisily

2. slowly

3. sudden

4. slightly

5. loud

6. quickly

7. safe

8. dangerous

9. Terrible

Part B

People cheered <u>loudly</u> as she spun around. The skater was <u>confident</u>. Suddenly, she jumped <u>high</u> in the air. She landed <u>easily</u>. Her <u>beautiful</u> costume sparkled under the lights. At the end of her act, she bowed and skated <u>quickly</u> to the sidelines.

Using Commas in a Series
Page 42
Part A

They saw fantastic, exciting, and incredible fireworks. Fireworks exploded, banged, and flashed in the sky. They looked so beautiful and bright. Everyone applauded as the fireworks boomed loudly and hissed faintly. After the show, Dan, Julie, and Sharon were hungry. They bought and ate hot dogs, potato chips, and lemonade.

Part B

Use these sentences to check your work. It's OK if your sentences are different from these. Just be sure that you used commas correctly.

1. I would like to own a station wagon, a sedan, and a sports car.

2. The car is old, rusty, and noisy.

3. The car rides smoothly, quietly, and comfortably.

Punctuating Letters
Page 43

3102 North Riverview Road
Chicago, IL 60657
July 2, 199_

Ms. Jean Hall
Laramie Publishing Company
202 North Truman Road
Chicago, IL 60601

Dear Ms. Hall:
Please send me a copy of *Careers in the Food Industry*. I have enclosed a check for $6.50.

Sincerely,

Lisa Byrd

Lisa Byrd

COMBINING SENTENCES

Using Conjunctions to Combine Sentences
Page 45

His family did not have a lot of money, <u>yet</u> he was still able to fulfill his dreams. Jackie Robinson went to Pasadena Junior College, <u>and</u> then he went to the University of California at Los Angeles. Robinson played many different sports in college, <u>and</u> he excelled in all of them. He had money problems during his junior year, <u>so</u> he had to drop out of college.

Robinson was a soldier during World War II, <u>and</u> then he joined an all-black baseball team called the Kansas City Monarchs. Branch Rickey was the president of the Brooklyn Dodgers, <u>and</u> he saw Robinson play. Rickey realized Robinson was a great player, <u>so</u> he asked him to join the Brooklyn farm team. Robinson had an outstanding batting average, <u>so</u> he was brought up to play for the Brooklyn Dodgers in 1947.

Racist fans sometimes booed Jackie Robinson, <u>but</u> he didn't let racism stop him. He later became active in the civil rights movement, <u>for</u> he believed in equality and freedom.

Using Connectors
Page 46

1. Dr. Sanders told Bart to eat foods low in fat; <u>moreover,</u> he said that Bart should avoid salty foods.

2. Bart used to eat fried foods; <u>however,</u> he now eats foods that are broiled or baked.

3. Bart doesn't like to exercise; <u>however,</u> he knows that working out will help him lose weight more quickly.

4. Bart walks a mile each day; <u>moreover,</u> he goes to the gym once a week and uses the exercise machines.

5. Bart is motivated; <u>therefore,</u> he will probably stick to his diet and exercise plan.

Using Subordinating Conjunctions
Page 47

1. Because she is a single parent,

2. before she goes to work

3. After Felicia leaves,

4. Although Felicia likes her job,

5. when (or because) Will is sick.

6. if (or when) her company opens a day-care center.

7. Although she likes the sitter,

8. because she will have more time with her son.

NEW TOPICS IN SENTENCE STRUCTURE

Identifying Misplaced Describing Phrases
Page 49

1. Shopping at discount markets, Esta saves money on groceries.

2. These markets, also called superstores, are popular in many cities and suburbs.

3. Esta reaches for cans stacked high on the shelves.

4. Esta gives coupons from the Sunday paper to the cashier.

Parallel Structure
Page 50

1. Moving to the suburbs and buying a home are Rafael's future plans.

2. He wants his children to play in safer parks and to go to better schools.

3. The mayor has not succeeded in improving education or lowering the crime rate.

4. Rafael believes that the city government is weak, dishonest, and uncaring.

Paragraph Structure
Page 51

1. **Topic sentence:** Cities in the United States grew for different reasons.
   Sentence off the topic: Many people like to visit Hollywood and search for their favorite movie stars.

2. **Topic sentence:** Helicopters have many uses.
   Sentence off the topic: Soldiers who fought in these wars were very brave.

3. **Topic sentence:** New laws are helping single parents collect child support.
   Sentence off the topic: Divorces are more common now than they were a hundred years ago.